The Greek Christmas Cookbook

Lucie Rogers

Contents

5 - Introduction

6 - Chicken Lemon and Egg Soup
7 - Spinach Pie
8 - Feta Cheese Triangles
9 - Fried Cheese
10 - Figs with Bacon
11 - Bulgar Wheat Salad
12 - Yogurt Dressing
13 - Cabbage Salad
14 - Bean Soup
16 - Feta Cheese and Roasted Red Pepper Dip
17 - Tomato Balls
18 - Artichoke Stew
19 - Fried Zucchini
20 - Tomato Slices with Oregano
21 - Green Beans
23 - Beetroot Salad
24 - Chickpea Soup
25 - Greek Pizza
26 - Roast Potatoes with Lemon
27 - Fried Salt Cod
29 - Crab Rolls
31 - Fish Patties
32 - Taramasalata
33 - Sea Bass with Olives
34 - Tuna Steaks
35 - Octopus in Red Wine
36 - Grape Leaves Stuffed With Meat
37 - Beef Roast with Lemon Gravy
40 - Pastitsio
43 - Stuffed Cabbage Rolls in Egg and Lemon Sauce
45 - Pork Chops
47 - Meatballs

48 - Roast Lamb
49 - Roast Turkey with Lemon and Oregano
53 - Pork with Olives
54 - Pilaf
55 - Chocolate Salami
56 - Christmas Bread
58 - Baklava
60 - Folded Pastries
62 - Olive Bread
63 - Custard Tart
64 - Honey Cookies
66 - Yogurt with Honey
67 - Chestnut Cake
68 - Spiced Quince
69 - Almond Cookies
70 - Rice Pudding
71 - Ricotta Pastries
72 - Tsipouro Christmas Cocktail
73 - Mulled Wine

75 - Photo Credits

Introduction

Christmas is a popular holiday in Greece. Christmas traditions are similar to those in other countries and include Christmas trees, Christmas fairs, carols and decorations.

Greece also has a number of unique Christmas traditions influenced by the Greek Orthodox Church and other Greek customs. These include decorating Christmas boats and fending off strange goblin creatures.

Food plays a big part in the Greek Christmas with Greek cookies, traditional Greek pies and pastries and typically Greek ingredients used in the Greek Christmas dinner.

Try some Greek Christmas food with the recipes in this book.

Chicken Lemon and Egg Soup

Ingredients

1 chicken
3 beaten eggs
90g/3.17 oz of uncooked rice
6 tablespoons of lemon juice
salt
black pepper

Put the chicken in a pot. Cover with water. Cover and boil then cook on a low heat for 1 hour.

Take the chicken and cut into pieces. Put the rice in the pot with the cooking liquid. Add some salt and pepper and cook on a low heat for 20 minutes until the rice is cooked.

Take off the heat.

Mix the eggs and lemon juice. Put some of the hot cooking liquid in the egg mix and whisk, then put the egg mix in the pot but off the heat. Whisk well, then add some salt and pepper.

Serve the soup with the chicken pieces.

Spinach Pie

Ingredients

400g/14.1 oz of spinach
250g/8.8 oz of crumbled feta cheese
1 finely chopped onion
2 tablespoons of fresh chopped parsley
1 tablespoon of chopped fresh dill
7g/0.3 oz of chopped fresh mint
pinch of nutmeg
2 eggs
olive oil
10 filo pastry sheets

Cook the onions in a pan in some olive oil for 6 minutes.

Add the spinach leaves and cook for 4 minutes. Add the parsley, dill, mint and nutmeg and cook for 2 minutes.

Mix the eggs with the crumbled feta cheese. Add to the spinach mix and add some more olive oil. Mix well.

Get a square baking dish a brush it with olive oil. Add a sheet of pastry and brush with olive oil Add more more pastry sheets brushed with oil. Spread over the spinach mix. Add the last 5 pastry sheets each brushed with olive oil. Cut into 10 squares in the dish - but do not cut all the way to the bottom of the baking dish.

Bake in preheated oven at 180C/350F. Cut into 10 pieces.

Feta Cheese Triangles

Ingredients

198g/7 oz of feta cheese
198g/7 oz of cream cheese
1 beaten egg
salt
black pepper
olive oil
filo pastry sheets

Mix the cheese, egg and some salt and pepper in a bowl.

Brush a filo sheet with olive oil. Put another sheet on top and brush with olive oil. Cut into 4cm/2 inch strips. Put some cheese mix on the end of the strip. Fold over to encase the cheese to make a triangle shape then keep going until the strip is used up. Repeat with the rest of the strips of the filo sheet, then repeat the process with more filo sheets.

Brush the triangle pastries with olive oil.

Put on a baking tray lined with parchment/greaseproof paper and cook in a preheated oven at 176C/350F for 25 minutes.

Fried Cheese

Ingredients

thick cheese slices such as Kefalograviera, Kasseri
halloumi or provalone
lemon juice
dried oregano
black pepper
flour
olive oil

Dip the cheese slices in cold water. Cold then in flour, Fry in hot oil in a pan until golden on each side.

Add some oregano. lemon juice and black pepper before serving.

Figs with Bacon

Ingredients

figs
bacon
goat's cheese

To make a fig with bacon, slice open a fig a put in a piece of goat's cheese. Wrap in bacon and secure with a wooden stick.

Place on a baking tray and cook broil/grill until the bacon is crisp.

Bulgar Wheat Salad

Ingredients

182g/1 cup of bulgar wheat
4 chopped spring onions/scallions
25g/1 cup of chopped parsley
280g/10 oz of chopped cherry tomatoes
50ml/1.7 fl oz of red wine vinegar
120ml/half a cup of olive oil
2 finely chopped cloves of garlic
salt
black pepper

Put the bulgar wheat in a bowl of hot water and leave for 25 minutes. Drain the bulgar wheat.

Mix the parsley, spring onions and cherry tomatoes. Add the bulgar.

Mix the olive oil, vinegar, garlic and some salt and pepper. Add to the bulgar wheat and mix.

Yogurt Dressing

Ingredients

4 tablespoons of olive oil
6 tablespoons of mayonnaise
2 teaspoon of finely chopped garlic
pinch of dried oregano
1 tablespoon of fresh dill
390g/12 oz of plain yogurt
3 tablespoons of lemon juice
pinch of salt

Gently mix the ingredients together in a bowl.

Cabbage Salad

Ingredients

350g/12.6 oz of shredded white cabbage
1 grated carrot
1 chopped red pepper
1 chopped stick of celery
3 tablespoons of red wine vinegar
1 tablespoon of olive oil
3 tablespoons of lemon juice
parsley
salt

Mix the cabbage, celery, carrot and pepper in a bowl.

Add some salt and squeeze the cabbage a little.

Mix the olive oil, lemon juice and vinegar. Add some chopped parsley to the salad and mix

Bean Soup

Ingredients

450g/1 lb of haricot/navy beans
6 finely chopped onions
1 chopped carrot
1 chopped celery stick
1 chopped clove of garlic
6 oz of tomato puree/paste
3 litres/12 and a half cups of water
salt
pepper
parsley
olive oil

Put the beans in a bowl of hot water for 35 minutes. Drain the beans.

Fry the onion, celery, carrot and garlic in some oil for 7 minutes. Add the water and tomato puree. Boil then add the beans and some salt and pepper.

Cook on a low heat for 2 hours - until the beans are cooked. Near the end of cooking add some fresh parsley.

Greek Christmas Facts

Christmas is called Christougena in Greece.

Christmas in Greece is celebrated on the 25th December.

A symbol of Christmas in Greece is the Christmas Boat - Karavaki. A boat is decorated for Christmas. This tradition is still carried out and there are Christmas boat decorations in most town squares.

The boats are decorated on 6th December which is St. Nicholas Day.

St. Nicholas is a patron Saint of fishermen and the boats were decorated to help make sure sailors and fishermen returned home safely for Christmas.

Greeks put up Christmas trees during the festive season.

The first Greek tree was decorated by Greek King Otto in 1933 at his palace. Otto was Bavarian and brought the German Christmas tree tradition to Greece.

Feta Cheese and Roasted Red Pepper Dip

Ingredients

226g/8 oz of feta cheese chunks
283g/10 oz of chopped roasted red bell peppers
1 chopped chilli pepper
chopped and pitted olives
chopped parsley
1 finely chopped clove of garlic
olive oil
1 tablespoon of lemon juice

Put the feta cheese, chilli, bell pepper, lemon juice, garlic and about 2 tablespoons of olive oil in a blender and blend.

When serving add some more olive oil, olives and parsley.

Tomato Balls

Ingredients

1 kg/2.2 lb of cherry tomatoes
74g/2.6 oz of chopped feta cheese
1 grated red onion
chopped parsley
chopped mint
1 teaspoon of dried oregano
65g/2.3 oz of flour
1 teaspoon of baking powder
salt
pepper
oil

Gently crush the tomatoes then put in a sieve. Place the sieve over a bowl and add some salt to the tomatoes.

Mix the tomatoes with the onion in a bowl. Add the feta cheese and some mint and parsley.

Mix the flour and baking powder with some salt and pepper. Add to the tomato and cheese mix. Make a dough. Put in a dough and refrigerate for 2 hours.

Make small balls from the dough and cook in hot oil for 3 minutes on each side. Place on paper towels to dry.

Artichoke Stew

Ingredients

6 peeled artichokes
1 litre/4 cups of water
3 tablespoons of flour
half a finely chopped onion
4 tablespoons of lemon juice
120ml/half a cup of olive oil
chopped dill
pinch of sugar
salt

Cook the onions in half the olive oil in a pan for 6 minutes.

Add the lemon juice, salt, sugar and the rest of the olive oil. Add the water and cover. Bring to the boil, then add the artichokes and some chopped dill. Cook on allow heat for 40 minutes.

Serve cooled.

Fried Zucchini

Ingredients

1 zucchini/courgette cut into long strips
295ml/10 fl oz carbonated water
1 cup of flour
olive oil
salt

Put the zucchini in a bowl and add some salt. Leave for 15 minutes. Drain.

Mix the water, some salt and the flour to make a batter.

Dip the zucchini in the batter and fry in hot oil for 6 minutes until golden brown.

Put on paper towels to drain.

Tomato Slices with Oregano

Ingredients

sliced tomatoes
olive oil
dried oregano
sea salt

Put the tomatoes on a plate. Drizzle with olive oil. Sprinkle on dried oregano and sea salt.

Green Beans

Ingredients

65ml/2.19 fl oz of olive oil
half a grated onion
453g/1 lb of green beans
4 crushed tomatoes
2 chopped tomatoes
1 tablespoon of tomato puree
1 peeled and chopped potato
salt
pepper

Cook the onion in the olive oil in a pan for 6 minutes.

Add the beans, stir and cook for 4 minutes.

Add the tomatoes, potatoes and some salt and pepper. Cover the beans with water. Cover and cook on a low heat for 25 minutes - until the potatoes are cooked.

Fried Cheese

Greek Pizza

Beetroot Salad

Ingredients

3 beetroot
1 clove of garlic
30g/1 oz of walnuts
250g/8.8 oz of Greek yogurt
olive oil
pepper
salt

Wash the beetroot and put in a pan of water. Bring to the boil then cook on a low heat for 30 minutes - until cooked. Peel and chop the beetroot.

Put the walnuts, garlic, some salt and pepper and some olive oil in a blender a make a smooth mix. Mix with the yogurt. Put this mix on top of the beetroot in a bowl and refrigerate for 1 hour.

Chickpea Soup

Ingredients

450g/1 lb of dried chickpeas
2 finely chopped onions
1 finely chopped clove of garlic
1 finely chopped carrots
1 bay leaf
fresh thyme
fresh dill
olive oil
3 tablespoons of lemon juice
800ml/3 and a quarter cups of water
salt
pepper

Soak the chickpeas for 10 hours.

Put the chickpeas in a pan of hot water anf boil for 11 minutes. Drain.

Fry the onions, celery, carrots and garlic in some olive oil in a saucepan for 8 minutes. Add the water, bay leaf chick peas and some thyme to the pot. Cook on a moderate heat for 35 minutes - until the chickpeas are cooked.

Add some salt and pepper, olive oil and lemon juice. Add some dill before serving.

Greek Pizza

Ingredients

chopped spinach
feta cheese
mozzarella cheese
pitted olives sliced in half
tomato slices
chopped onion
pizza dough
dried oregano
black pepper
lemon juice
finely chopped garlic
olive oil
salt
pepper

Roll out the dough and make a pizza base. Brush with olive oil and top with the rest of the ingredients.

Put pizza on a baking tray and cook in a preheated oven at 200C/400F for 20 minutes.

Roast Potatoes with Lemon

Ingredients

1.2 kg/2.8 lb of wedge cut potatoes
olive oil
6 tablespoons of lemon juice
salt
1 teaspoon of dried oregano
black pepper
600ml/2 and a half cups of chicken stock/broth

Put the potatoes in a bowl and mix with the lemon juice and some olive oil. Add some salt and pepper and the oregano and mix.

Put the potatoes in a baking pan. Add the chicken stock/broth. Cook in a preheated oven at 200C/400F until cooked - about 1 hour 10 minutes.

Fried Salt Cod

Ingredients

680g/1 and a half lb of dried salt cod
120g/1 cup of flour
salt
a teaspoon of baking powder
oil
pepper

Soak the cod in water for 5 hours. Change the water 3 times. Drain the cod and cut into 8 pieces.

Mix the flour, baking powder and some salt and pepper. Add some water and make a batter. dip the cod in the batter and fry in hot oil until crispy.

Greek Christmas Facts

During Christmas Greeks are scared of evil spirits named the Kallikantzaroi. These are goblin like creatures with long thin limbs that try to cut down the tree that hold the Earth so the Earth will collapse. But just as they are about to complete sawing the tree down the Christmas period starts and they are able to come to Earth. They forget about the tree and cause mischief playing tricks on people between December 25 and January 6th.

They have to return underground on January 6th - Epiphany - and find that the tree has regenerated so have to start the process of sawing it down again.

A famous Christmas in Greece is the one put up in Syntagma Square in Athens.

Greek Christmas carols are called Kalanda in Greek. There are three caroling days where carols are sung: Christmas Eve 24th December; New Years Eve morning 31st December and the morning of the Eve of Epiphany 5th January.

In Greece children sing carols with drums and metal triangles. They are rewarded with money and cookies.

Greek Christmas carols normally wish luck and prosperity to families.

Crab Rolls

Ingredients

3 chopped mushrooms
half a finely chopped onion
2 tablespoons of flour
500ml/1 pint of warm milk
chopped parsley
chopped dill
75g/half a cup of dry breadcrumbs
filo pastry sheets
butter
salt
pepper

Cook the onions in butter for 6 minutes. Add the flour and make a paste. Add the milk and stir to make a thick sauce.

Take off the heat and add the crab, mushrooms, breadcrumbs and some parsley, dill and salt and pepper. Mix.

Put three sheets of filo on a surface and add a tablespoon of mix. Make a roll. Repeat with the rest of the crabmeat.

Put on a baking sheet, brush some melted butter on top and cook in a preheated oven at 187C/370F for 45 minutes.

Chicken Lemon and Egg Soup

Taramasalata

Fish Patties

Ingredients

1.3 kg/3 lb of whole fish such as cod
80g/2.82 oz of kefalotyri or Parmesan cheese
1 chopped stick of celery
1 onion cut into half
half a finely chopped onion
28g/1 oz
2 eggs
chopped mint
chopped parsley
150g/1 cup of dry breadcrumbs
flour
oil
lemon juice
salt
pepper

Boil a saucepan of water. Add the halved onion, celery and some parsley. Boil for 11 minutes. Add the fish, cover and cook on a low heat for 20 minutes.

Drain the liquid and keep. Remove the bones, head and skin from the fish. Keep the flesh.

Put the fish in a bowl and flake. Add the eggs, onion, finely chopped onion, mint, salt and pepper, cheese and 120ml/half a cup of water.

Make into patty shapes and coat in flour. Fry in hot oil until browned. Add some lemon juice before serving.

Taramasalata

Ingredients

130g/4.5 oz of cod roe
half a finely chopped onion
5 tablespoons of lemon juice
4 slices of white bread
130ml/half a cup of olive oil

Put the onion, cod roe and lemon juice in a blender and make a paste.

Remove the crusts from the bread. Put the bread in some water and then squeeze. Add to the other ingredients in the blender and blend again. Add the olive oil to the blender and mix again.

Sea Bass with Olives

Ingredients

4 sea bass fillets
1 clove of finely chopped garlic
3 tablespoons of pine nuts
10 pitted olives
3 tablespoons of lemon juice
fresh chopped oregano
olive oil
salt
pepper

Put some salt and pepper on the fish. Cook the fish skin side down in hot olive oil in a pan for 3 minutes. Turn the fish over and cook for 2 minutes. Put the fish on a plate.

Put some more olive oil in a pan and cook the pine nuts and garlic for 2 minutes. Add the olives and cook for another minute.

Take off the heat and stir in the lemon juice. Leave for 1 minute then add the oregano and mix. Serve this sauce over the bass.

Tuna Steaks

Ingredients

4 tuna steaks
lemon slices
1 teaspoon of dried oregano
1 teaspoon of dried thyme
salt
pepper
olive oil

Mix the oregano and thyme with some olive oil and salt and pepper. Rub the mix on the tuna. Put the tune in a bowl, cover and refrigerate for 25 minutes.

Put some olive oil in a pan and heat. Cook the tuna for 5 minutes on each side. Serve with lemon slices.

Octopus in Red Wine

Ingredients

1.8 lb of octopus cut into chunks
3 chopped onions
240ml/1 cup of red wine
1 bay leaf
olive oil
salt
pepper

Cook the onions in some olive oil in a saucepan for 7 minutes.

Put the octopus, bayleaf and some sat and pepper in the pan. Put the wine in the pan and enough water to cover the octopus. Boil then cover the pan and cook on a low heat for 55 minutes - until the octopus is cooked.

Grape Leaves Stuffed With Meat

Ingredients

396g/14 oz of minced/ground beef
198g/7 oz of minced/ground lamb
141g/5 oz of rice
half a finely chopped onion
chopped fresh parsley
60g/2.11 oz of pine nuts
1 finely chopped garlic clove
1 teaspoon of chopped fresh mint
1 tablespoon of lemon juice
yogurt
414ml/14 fl oz of beef stock/broth
grape leaves

Put the meat, half the beef stock, onion, pine nuts, garlic, rice, mint and parsley in a bowl and mix.

Put a tablespoon of meat mix in the middle of a grape leaf. Roll it up. Repeat until the meat mix is used up.

Put the grape leaves in a pan. Add the rest of the stock and the lemon juice.

Cover the leaves with a plate then simmer for 50 minutes.

Beef Roast with Lemon Gravy

Ingredients

1.3kg/2.86lb beef joint
16 cloves of garlic
2 finely chopped onions
70ml/2.3 fl oz of white wine
1 peeled carrot
2 bay leaves
sprig of rosemary
1 tablespoon of lemon zest
5 tablespoons of lemon juice
cornflour/cornstarch
butter

Make 7 cuts in the beef and add a garlic clove and some salt and pepper to each cut.

Heat up some olive oil in a cooking pot. Cook the beef on all sides for a few minutes to brown. Put the beef on a plate.

Put the onions in the pan and cook for 10 minutes on a medium heat. Add the rest of the garlic, lemon juice, wine, lemon zest, carrot, rosemary and bay leaves. Put the beef back in the pot and cook until the wine and alcohol smell is gone.

Cover the beef with hot water. Add a little salt and pepper and the carrot. Cook on a low heat for 3 hours - until the meat is cooked.

Put the beef on a plate; remove the rosemary, carrot and bay leaves.

Mix 4 tablespoons of corn flour with water and add to the pan. Then cook over a medium heat stirring all the time until the sauce has thickened. Remove from heat a mix in a tablespoon of butter.

Cut the beef into slices and serve with the sauce.

Greek Christmas Facts

Saint Basil is Santa Claus in Greece. Agios Vasilis is Saint Basil in Greek. On New Years Eve a Saint Basil's Cake is served and whoever finds a coin in the cake is granted luck in the New Year.

When the Saint Basil's cake is cut a slice is made for Christ, the Virgin Mary, the house and then slices for the people in the house.

Saint Basil has a white beard and red cape. On 1st January - Saint Basil's feast day - gifts are exchanged by Greeks and Saint Basil gives gifts to children.

Kourabiedes are a traditional Christmas cookie in Greece. Listed in this book as Almond Cookies, the cookie originated in Ottoman times.

Melomakarona Cookies - Honey Cookies - in this book are another popular Christmas cookie. These cookies have their roots in the Byzantine era.

Pomegranate is a popular Christmas decoration in Greece. In Greece the fruit is a symbol of prosperity, fortune and fertility.

Pastitsio

Ingredients

700g/1.5 lb of minced/ground beef
2 finely chopped cloves of garlic
2 finely chopped onions
80g/2.8 oz of grated halloumi cheese
2 tablespoons of tomato puree/paste
1 teaspoon of cinnamon
1 cinnamon stick
1 bay leaf
135ml of red wine
1 chopped tomato
230ml/7.7 fl oz of beef stock/broth
330ml/11 fl oz of small pasta tubes - e.g. bucatini
fresh chopped parsley
1 beaten egg
olive oil

topping

140g/5 oz of butter
140g/5 oz of flour
1.3 litres.2 and a half pints of milk
nutmeg
2 beaten eggs
sea salt
black pepper

Fry the garlic and onion in some oil for 8 minutes. Add the tomato puree and cook for a few minutes then add the beef mince and some cinnamon powder. Cook for a few minutes and stir. Add the bay leaf, wine and cinnamon stick. Boil then cook for 7 minutes to reduce the wine. Remove the cinnamon stick and bay leaf.

Add the tomato and stock. Boil then cook on a low heat for 30 minutes.

Put the pasta in a pan of boiling salted water and cook for about 8 minutes - do not cook the pasta completely. Drain the pasta and coat with olive oil. Mix in the egg, some of the cheese and some parsley.

For the topping melt the butter and add the flour to make a paste. Stir in the milk and make a sauce. Cook on a low heat until the sauce thickens. Add half the halloumi cheese and some nutmeg. Add the eggs and mix.

Put half of the pasta mix in a baking dish. Add half of the beef sauce. Add the rest of he pasta and then the beef sauce. Top with the topping sauce and the rest of the cheese.

Cook in a preheated oven at 180/356FC for 45 minutes - until browned.

Honey Cookies

Chocolate Salami

Stuffed Cabbage Rolls in Egg and Lemon Sauce

Ingredients

453g/1 lb of minced/ground beef
1 cabbage with core removed
230g/8. 11 oz of shirt grain rice
1 grated onion
1 grated carrot
1 finely chopped spring onion
2 tablespoons of fresh chopped dill
2 tablespoons of chopped fresh parsley
olive oil
sea salt
black pepper
4 and a half cups of chicken stock
sliced lemon

for egg and lemon sauce

1 egg
2 egg yolks
quart
3 tablespoons of lemon juice
2 teaspoons of cornflour/cornstarch

Put the rice, onion, spring onion, carrot, beef, dill, parsley in a pan with some salt, pepper and olive oil. Put in a bowl and refrigerate for 30 minutes.

Put the cabbage in a pan of boiling salted water. Put the cabbage in the pan and cook on a medium heat for 15 minutes until the cabbage leaves come apart easily. Drain the cabbage. Separate the cabbage into leaves.

Put spoonfuls of the rice/beef mix on the cabbage rolls. Roll up the cabbage leaves and enclose the rice mix. Layer the cabbage rolls in a saucepan seam side down. Pour the chicken stock in the pan. Add some salt and pepper. Bring to the boil, cover then cook on a low heat for 45 minutes until the rice is cooked.

Remove the cabbage rolls and keep the water in the pan.

For the egg and lemon sauce mix the eggs. Add the cornflour and lemon and mix. Put three tablespoons of hot water from the pan in the egg mix and whisk. Put the egg mix in the pan of water. Cook on a medium heat for 2 minutes.

Add some salt and pepper.

Serve the sauce with the cabbage rolls.

Pork Chops

Ingredients

4 pork chops
5 potatoes cut into pieces
olive oil
4 tablespoons of lemon juice
1 chopped red onion
6 teaspoons of dried oregano
3 tablespoons of dry white wine
2 chopped clove of garlic
salt
pepper

Put the onions, half the garlic and pork chops in a bowl. Add half the lemon juice and some olive and salt and pepper. Add half the oregano and mix. Cover and refrigerate for 2 hours.

Line a baking tray with greaseproof/parchment paper. Put the potatoes on top and add some olive oil and half the lemon juice. Sprinkle over the wine and the other half of the garlic and oregano. Put a damp piece of greaseproof/parchment paper on top and seal in the potatoes. cook in a preheated oven at 175C/347F for 50 minutes.

Cook the pork chops in a hot frying pan in olive oil for 2 minutes on each side. Put the pork chops in the greasproof/parchment paper on top of the potatoes and cook for 15 minutes - until cooked.

Put the pork chops on a plate, cover with foil and leave for 15 minutes. Remove the greaseproof/parchment paper from the top of the potatoes and cook them for another 15 minutes.

Meatballs

Ingredients

396gg/14 oz of minced/ground beef
396g/14 oz of grated onion
60g/2.11 oz of breadcrumbs
1 teaspoon of lemon juice
1 teaspoon of dried mint
flour
half a teaspoon of dried oregano
oil
salt
pepper

Mix some salt with the onion, put in a colander and put some cold water on it. Squeeze the onion. Add the beef, breadcrumbs, oregano, mint, lemon juice and some salt and pepper.

Get a tablespoon of the beef mix and form into a ball. Roll in flour. Repeat for the rest of the meat mix.

Fry in hot oil until golden brown.

Roast Lamb

Ingredients

1 lamb shoulder
5 cloves of garlic
olive oil
8 tomatoes
5 peeled carrots
fresh sage
fresh thyme prigs
fresh rosemary
salt
pepper

Cut small slices slices in the meat and put garlic cloves in them. Rub with olive oil and season with salt and pepper.

Put the meat in a hot frying pan with some oil and cook on each side for about 3 minutes to brown.

Put the carrots, tomatoes and some sage and rosemary in a casserole dish. Put the lamb in and top with some thyme. Cover and cook in a preheated oven at 160C/320F for 4 hours - until cooked.

Remove the lamb. Take the rosemary, sage and thyme out of the pan and mash the tomatoes. Serve the dish juices with shredded lamb.

Roast Turkey with Lemon and Oregano

Ingredients

1 turkey
butter

stuffing

3 tablespoons of lemon juice
4 finely chopped onions
280g/9.8 oz of white bread cut into pieces
fresh chopped parsley
3 tablespoons of chopped fresh oregano
2 tablespoons of lemon zest

salt
pepper
nutmeg

For the stuffing, fry the onions in some oil for 8 minutes. Put the bread, parsley and oregano in a blender and make breadcrumbs. Add the breadcrumbs to the pan with the onion. Add the lemon zest and some salt and pepper.

Stuff the turkey with the stuffing.

Smear butter on the turkey, add some salt, pepper and nutmeg and put tin foil on top. Cook the turkey in a preheated oven at 190C/374F for 20 minutes per kilogram/2.2 lb, plus 90 minutes.

Take the tin foil off 90 minutes before the end of cooking.

Greek Christmas Facts

On Christmas Eve Christmas Bread - Christopsome - is baked. Regions have different variations on the recipe.

Often the decoration on the top reflects the livelihood of the family.

Christmas in Greece is influenced by the Greek Orthodox Church and local traditions.

Christmas in Greece starts around the start of December with traditional Christmas markets and fairs and Christmas food and drink.

In Greece Christmas runs between 24th December until Epiphany on the 6th January.

Gifts are traditionally given to children on New Year's Day in Greece.

In modern times families have started to give gifts on Christmas Day - December 25th, or both December 25th and 1st January.

Baklava

Christmas Bread

Pork with Olives

Ingredients

816/1.8 lb pork tenderloin cut into slices
11 destoned olives
1 sliced onion
170g/6 oz of sliced mushrooms
1 finely chopped clove of garlic
240ml/1 cup of white wine (dry)
chopped mint
chopped parsley
butter
salt
pepper

Brown the pork and garlic in butter a large saucepan for 6 minutes.

Add the onion, mushrooms, wine and some salt, pepper, mint and parsley.

Cover the pan and cook on a low heat for 50 minutes until the pork is cooked.

Add the olives and cook for another 6 minutes.

Pilaf

Ingredients

1 chicken cut into pieces
1 cup/210g of uncooked long grain rice
1 chopped onion
7 tablespoons of butter
black pepper
pinch of cinnamon
pinch of allspice
salt
2 tablespoons of tomato puree/paste

Put some butter in a saucepan with the chicken, cinnamon, allspice and some salt and pepper. Cook for 3 minutes to brown the chicken.

Add the onions and cook for 5 minutes. Add the tomato puree and 2 tablespoons of water. Cover the pan and cook on a low heat for 22 minutes.

Add the rice and 500ml/2 cups of hot water. Cover and cook on a low heat for 22 minutes - until the chicken is cooked.

Chocolate Salami

Ingredients

230g/8.11 oz of dark/bittersweet chocolate
100g/3.5 oz of butter
170g/6 oz of plain biscuits/cookies
45g/1.5 oz of chopped walnuts
milk
icing/powdered sugar

Put the chocolate and butter in a glass bowl. Put the bowl over a pot of water on a medium heat and melt stirring all the time.

Add the biscuits, walnuts and a little milk and mix.

Put the chocolate mix on a piece of clingfilm/plastic sheet. Roll into a log shape. Put in the freezer for one hour. Roll once more, remove the wrap and dust with sugar. Slice to serve.

Christmas Bread

Ingredients

60g/2.11 oz of chopped walnuts
240g/8.4 oz of sugar
4 eggs
240ml/1 cup of milk
2 and a half tablespoons of yeast
1 teaspoon of vanilla essence/extract
170g/6 oz of melted butter
1 teaspoon of nutmeg
1 teaspoon of cinnamon
1 teaspoon of dried star anise
800g/1.7 lb of flour
130ml of warm water
1 teaspoon of grated lemon zest
salt

Mix the yeast, water, 1 tablespoon of flour, 1 teaspoon of sugar and a pinch of salt n a bowl. Leave in a warm place for 12 minutes.

Warm the milk then leave to cool.

Mix the sugar, 3 of the eggs milk, yeast mix and a pinch of salt in a bowl. Add the flour, vanilla, butter, walnuts, cinnamon, star anise, nutmeg and lemon peel and mix to make a dough.

Knead the dough for 7 minutes. Put wrap in clingfilm/plastic wrap and put in a bowl. Cover with a damp towel and leave in a warm place for 1 hour.

Knead a little again, then wrap in plastic wrap and cover with a damp towel and leave for 30 minutes.

Cut a quarter of the dough off. Roll this piece into four rope like shapes. Braid two pieces of dough together and then braid the other two pieces. Put these two braids on the top of the other dough ball to form a cross. Put in a cake tin lined with greaseproof/parchment paper. Leave for 1 hour.

Cook in a preheated oven at 276C/350F for 40 minutes - until cooked.

Baklava

Ingredients

filo pastry sheets
396g/14 oz of chopped nuts
200g/7 oz of melted butter
1 teaspoon of cinnamon
230ml/7.7 fl oz of water
180g/6.3 oz of sugar
1 teaspoon of vanilla extract
30g/1 oz of honey

Mix the nuts and cinnamon.

Butter a rectangular baking dish. Put 8 sheets of filo pastry in the pan, buttering each filo pastry sheet. Add some nuts and add 2 sheets of filo pastry buttering each sheet. Repeat the layers and finish with 6 layers of filo pastry. Cut 4 x 3 pieces in the pan. Put in a preheated oven at 175C/350F.

Put the sugar and water in pan and bring to the boil. Boil for 5 minutes. Add the honey and vanilla extract and cook on a low heat for 25 minutes.

Take the dish out of the oven and pour the warm sugar syrup over the top. Leave to cool.

Greek Christmas Facts

6th January - Epiphany is the end of Christmas in Greece.

The Greek Christmas dinner is on Christmas Day, December 25th.

The dinner includes:

roasted meat
pies
numerous side dishes such as vegetable dishes

Avgolemono - Chicken, Lemon and Egg Soup - is a popular starter for the Greek Christmas dinner.

The main course is roast meat such as roast pork, beef with lemon sauce, turkey or lamb.

Cabbage rolls are a widely prepared side dish.

Turkey is not a common dish in Greece but has become a popular choice for Christmas dinner.

Folded Pastries

Ingredients

340g/12 oz of flour
4 egg yolks
1 egg
2 tablespoons of melted butter
60ml/a quarter of a cup of orange juice
1 teaspoon of baking powder
oil
honey
water
chopped walnuts
cinnamon powder

Mix the flour and baking powder.

Mix the egg yolks and egg. Mix the egg with the butter and orange juice. Add the flour and mix to make a dough. knead for 10 minutes.

Make four pieces from the dough. Put on a baking tray and cover with clingfilm/plastic wrap. Leave for 30 minutes.

For the syrup heat some honey and water together in a pan until a syrup is made.

Roll the dough pieces into smaller rectangular sheets. Cut the sheets into smaller rectangles about the size of a biscuit/cookie.

Fry in oil until golden brown.

Top the pastries with syrup, cinnamon and walnuts before serving.

Olive Bread

Ingredients

160g/5.6 oz of chopped olives
210ml/7.1 fl oz of warm water
2 and a half teaspoons of yeast
420g/3 and a half cups of flour
sea salt
half a tablespoon of sugar
2 tablespoons of olive oil

Put the yeast in the warm water and leave for 7 minutes.

Mix the flour, olive oil, sugar and a little sea salt in a bowl.
Add the yeast and make a dough. Knead for 18 minutes,

Firm the dough into a ball and place on a greased baking
tray. Cover with a damp towel and leave for 45 minutes to
rise.

Add the olives to the dough and knead for another 7
minutes.

Divide the dough into 4 pieces and make into round
shapes. Put on a baking sheet with flour on and cut some
slices in the top. Cover with a damp towel and leave in a
warm place for 25 minutes.

Cook in a preheated oven at 201C/390F for 22 minutes.

Custard Tart

Ingredients

1 litre/4 cups of milk
11 tablespoons of semolina
210g/7.4 oz
4 eggs
1 tablespoon of vanilla extract
half a tablespoon of lemon zest
1 tablespoon of butter
icing/confectioners' sugar
cinnamon

Mix the sugar, semolina, lemon zest zest, vanilla extract, 1 cup of the milk and 3 of the eggs in a bowl.

Put the rest of the milk in a pan. Bring to the boil, then add to the other mixture. Whisk well then put back in the pan. Cook over a low heat for 11 minutes stirring all the time. Take off the heat and mix in the butter. Leave to cool for several minutes.

Grease a large tart/cake tin. Add the mix. Beat the last egg and put this on top. Cook in a preheated oven at 176C/350F for 50 minutes. Cool then dust with icing sugar and cinnamon.

Honey Cookies

Ingredients

dough

100ml/3.3 fl oz of orange juice
220ml/7.4 fl oz of olive oil
40g/1.41 oz of honey
70ml/2.3 fl oz of water
80g/2.82 oz of sugar
1 teaspoon of cinnamon
pinch of nutmeg
drop of vanilla extract
1 teaspoon of lemon zest
100g/3.52 oz of semolina
500g/1.1 lb of self raising flour

for glaze

500g/1.1 lb of sugar
80g/2.82 oz of honey
400ml/1 and three quarters of a cup of water
1 cinnamon stick
1 tablespoon of orange peel

chopped walnuts

Put all the dough ingredients apart from the flour and semolina in a bowl. Mix well. Add the semolina and flour and make a dough.

Put the dough in a bowl and cover with a damp tea towel

and leave for 30 minutes.

Put the glaze ingredients in a pan and boil then simmer for 5 minutes.

Roll the dough into balls then make into cookie shapes and put on a baking tray lined with parchment/greaseproof paper. Cut a couple of lines in the top of each cookie. Cook in a preheated oven at 185C/365F for 22 minutes.

Dip the cookies in the glaze. Put some chopped walnuts on top.

Yogurt with Honey

Ingredients

Greek yogurt
walnuts
honey

Put some yogurt in a bowl. Add some walnuts. Drizzle honey over the top.

Chestnut Cake

Ingredients

240g/1 cup of chestnut puree
240ml/1 cup of whipped cream
1 teaspoon of vanilla extract
6 egg yolks
6 egg whites
240g/8.4 oz
40g/1.4 oz of chopped almonds
salt

Mix the egg yolk and sugar to make a smooth paste. Mix in the chestnut puree, almonds and vanilla.

Mix the egg whites and a little salt to make a stiff mix. Add to the other mix.

Put into greased cake tins and cook in a preheated oven at 160C/320F for 40 minutes.

Cut the cakes in half and spread cream in the middle and on the top of the cakes.

Spiced Quince

Ingredients

1.8kg/4 lb of cored, peeled and sliced quince
1.8kg/4 lb of sugar
1.08/litres/4 and a half cups of water
50ml/1.7 fl oz of lemon juice + extra
1 cinnamon stick
1 teaspoon of lemon peel
1 teaspoon of vanilla essence
walnuts

Put the water in a pan. Add the quince. Boil then cover and cook on a low heat for 25 minutes - until soft. Drain and reserve about 200ml/6.7 fl oz of the cooking liquid.

Take the pot of the heat. Put layers of quince and sugar and cooking liquid in the pan and leave for 2 hours.

Put the pan on the heat and add the vanilla, lemon peel and cinnamon stick. Boil then cook on a low heat until the mix has thickened. Take off the heat and add a few tablespoons of lemon juice. Cool then store in jars.

Serve with walnuts.

Almond Cookies

Ingredients

95g/3.3 oz of chopped blanched almonds
200g/7 oz of self raising flour
200g/7 oz of butter
1 egg yolk
drop of vanilla extract
1 tablespoon of orange juice or brandy
icing/confectioners' sugar
flour

Mix the butter and sugar to make a paste. Add the egg, orange juice/brandy and vanilla extract. Whisk together then add the almonds. Add the flour and mix well to make a dough. Put in the refrigerator for 30 minutes.

Form into crescent shapes about 2.5 cm/1 inch in size. Put into individual paper cookie moulds. Bake in a preheated oven at 170C/325F for 30 minutes. Dust with icing sugar.

Rice Pudding

Ingredients

110g/half a cup of uncooked short grain rice
620ml/1.3 pints of milk
4 and a half tablespoons of sugar
4 tablespoons of cornflour/cornstarch
1 teaspoon of vanilla extract
cinnamon

Mix the cornstarch with some of the milk.

Put the rice in a pan with 500ml/2 cups of water. Bring to a boil then simmer for 35 minutes.

Add the rest of the milk and sugar and bring to a boil. Add the cornflour mix and vanilla extract and stir. Put into bowls and add some cinnamon. Refrigerate for 3 hours before serving.

Ricotta Pastries

Ingredients

375g/1 and half cups of ricotta cheese
113g/4 oz of feta cheese
512g/4 cups of flour
2 tablespoons of grappa or apple brandy
olive oil
salt
fresh thyme
honey

Mix the feta and ricotta.

Mix the flour, grappa, 240ml/1 cup of water, 2 tablespoons of olive oil and some salt and make a dough. Put in a bowl, cover with clingfilm and leave for 35 minutes.

Roll out the dough into a rectangle and cut into about 12 strips. Put about 3 tablespoons of the cheese mix on the long side of a strip and roll the strip up from the longest side. Seal the pastries to enclose the filling.

Fry in olive oil for 7 minutes on each side - until golden brown.

Tsipouro Christmas Cocktail

Ingredients

tsipouro
whisky
brown sugar
apple slices
cloves

Put some whisky, tsipouro, brown sugar, apple slices and some cloves in a bowl. seal the bowl and leave in the dark for a few days.

Put all the ingredients apart from the apples in a pan with some water. Bring to a boil. Cool then add the apple slices. Leave for 1 and a half hours before straining.

Mulled Wine

Ingredients

red wine
honey

Put some wine and honey in a pan and simmer for 10 minutes. Leave for 30 minutes. Warm in the pan before serving.

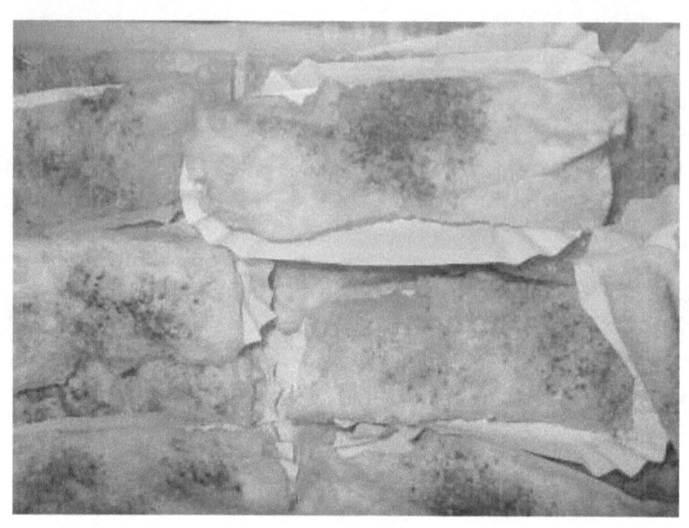

Folded Pastries

Photo Credits

Fried Cheese

https://commons.wikimedia.org/wiki/File:Sagknaki_frie
d_cheese.jpg

Leeturtle

1 September 2021

Folded Pastries

https://commons.wikimedia.org/wiki/File:2011_Greek_
Diples.JPG

Richard Arthur Norton

16 May 2011

Baklava

https://commons.wikimedia.org/wiki/File:Baklava_kymi
_greece.jpg

Mari Beika

18 August 2014

Christmas Bread

https://commons.wikimedia.org/wiki/File:Christopsomo

_-_Greek_Christmas_Bread_-_Flickr_-_pellaea.jpg

Jason Hollinger

25 December 2011

Taramosalata

https://commons.wikimedia.org/wiki/File:Taramosalata 01.jpg

Robert Kindermann

29 July 2006

Chicken Lemon and Egg Soup

https://commons.wikimedia.org/wiki/File:Avgolemono_ soup.jpg

robin.norwood

10 October 2008

Greek Pizza

https://en.wikipedia.org/wiki/List_of_Greek_dishes#/m edia/File:Greek_pizza.jpg

katharine j moriarty

5 September 2008

Chocolate Salami

https://en.wikipedia.org/wiki/List_of_Greek_dishes#/media/File:Salame_de_chocolate_-_Chocolat_Salami.jpg

jppaguilar

23 November 2014

Honey Cookies

https://en.wikipedia.org/wiki/List_of_Greek_dishes#/media/File:Melomakarona.jpg

Kalambaki2

24 December 2011

Christmas Boat

https://commons.wikimedia.org/wiki/File:Xmas_ship1.JPG

Templar52

22 December 2006

Front Cover

https://commons.wikimedia.org/wiki/File:Athens_Christmas_Tree.jpg

George E. Koronaios

6 January 2019